AWAKENING

AWAKENING

Being One with His Bridal Proposal

Christine Nelson

First published in 2019.

AWAKENING
Being one with His bridal proposal

ISBN: 978-1-910986-17-2 (Kindle)
ISBN: 978-1-910986-18-9 (Paperback)

CN Publishing House
Kemp House,
152-160 City Road
London
EC1V 2NX

Visit our website at www.cnpublishinghouse.com
CN Publishing House is a division of Christine Nelson Enterprises

**Dr. Christine Nelson
(Author)**

CONTENTS

DEDICATION

I would like to dedicate this book to our Bridegroom, the Lover of my Soul, Who in many ways has saved me from myself. Your thoughts towards me have ravished my heart. Your words to me have been life transforming. Thank You for doing all the work so I can benefit. Thank You that no good thing will You withhold from me. Your foresight to consider all my needs and meeting them in advance has empowered me to enter Your rest. Thank You for being my constant Supply within me. I love Your extravagant love for me that says nothing is too hard for You to do for me because I am invaluable to You. Thank You for making me know that I am the daughter You love.

ACKNOWLEDGEMENTS

Thank you so much to the partners of *CNMinistries - Revealing the Christ in You*. I am super grateful to all the students at *CNM Apostolic Equipping Institute* (or CNMAEI) for all your support. I am forever grateful to you all. Thank you for being my sound board; my first audience.

Thank you, Gail Ingram for your patience and your editorial suggestions.

Thank you to Pamela Jones for capturing, in the Spirit, the very essence of this book, *Being One with His Proposal* by painting the cover.

Thank you to Karizmatik Media Ltd for doing the book cover.

Thank you to Pura Track for formatting.

INTRODUCTION

Awakening to His love

I t is every little girl's dream to know what it feels like to be proposed to. It is every little boy's dream to hear the gleeful, "YES! YES!" that responds to that proposal. The day of the proposal is a memorable day, and many will say life transforming. It is a day when commitment is made between the potential bride and groom.

This commitment could not be had without the agreement of both parties. In the Spirit, we see that our Bridegroom, Jesus, makes an unconditional commitment to us, His Bride, by presenting to us a love like no other. It is a love that carries no strings or conditions and is not reflective of our acceptance nor our attitude nor even our behaviour; incredible!

He unveils to us His heart towards us and demonstrates it by the infinite lengths in which He goes, having put in place for us to know He has loved us from eternity. He reveals His foresight by putting us in Himself from the foundation of the world so that we have all we need to live out His commitment as our own. His desire for us is revealed as He shows by loving us, over and over, that He does nothing out of duty or because He has to; even when we look through our own eyes and think we are unlovable. We are enveloped by His love as we see over and over again that through His eyes, we are perfect. When we look through His eyes of faith, we are blameless, innocent, holy, complete.

AWAKENING: Being One with His Bridal Proposal was written to captivate the hearts of believers to know the heart of our Amazing God towards us: how He has been romancing us throughout the ages as His very own. It awakens us to a love walk that is devoid of fear, duty, law, or a will power driven initiative, causing us to be aware of a GRACE LIFE that points back to our Beloved Bridegroom, Jesus. Beyond our earthly parents, beyond our family bloodline, we are called to gaze deeply into the complete fulfilment of this wondrous love revealed to us through our Redeemer.

As you read be sure to allow your heart to be

wooed and swooped up in the endless intimacy with your FIRST TRUE LOVE: Jesus.

So we pray: *Father, we thank you for the Gift of Grace, Gift of Innocence, the Gift of Perfection, the Gift of Love, Gift of Holiness, the Gift of a Pure Heart, the Gift of Mercy, the Gift of Redemption, the Gift of Kindness, the Gift of Humility, the Gift of Peace, the Gift of Righteousness. These and more that are encompassed in our wonderful Bridegroom Jesus and NOW in us by His grace. Thank You. Thank You.*

Chapter 1

AWAKENING TO HIS HEART

It is a matter of the heart

In recent years, I have gone through some of the most turbulent times in my marriage. So much so, it has left me wondering if the new year would find me in this twenty plus year marriage. The pain I have experienced within my heart has been alive and well. It has been so profound that I was not awakened by the light peering through the blinds of my window, nor the small footsteps of my 7-year-old but the dulled yet piercing pain within my heart. It was an overwhelming pain that seemed to be highlighted even more as I slept.

Feeling alone and abandoned, one of the days in my grief, I turned to the Father in frustration; I demanded pointedly, "How can You relate to me in this time of great pain?" Our Father spoke to me in a gentle voice. He shared that He sent His Only Son to pay the ultimate price for His bride. However, though the price has been paid in full, wrong beliefs, human reasoning and religious ideologies about the Godhead have caused many to treat the Bridegroom with apathy, disdain, half-hearted measures, or the dutiful attitude of a Pharisaic heart. All or any of these can cause (less than ideal), even loveless marriage relationships between many. He expressed how His Son gave of Himself willingly and wholeheartedly to His bride by the extent of His sacrifice; yet, many are still waiting for another bridegroom or have settled for an earthly bridegroom rather than our Heavenly Bridegroom. As a result, many have a dating relationship rather than deciding on a steadfast, devoted relationship. As I listened to His voice, I saw the lack of commitment He spoke of, as something I too have experienced. I know the heart break very well. He expressed His desire for the Bride of Christ to move from **Chav** to **Racham**: from a heart wrenching one-sided relationship to a two-sided intrinsic love relationship.

The Bible describes two types of love demonstrated within scripture. In John 3:16 the Bible reads:

> *"for God so loved the world that He gave His*

only begotten Son that whosoever believes in Him will have everlasting life".

The word *love* in this scripture, according to Hebrew scholars, refers to a love that is not returned. This love is one-sided, the Hebrew word **Chav.** This love many of us have experienced: we have given ourselves wholly to someone we love, we have gone the extra mile and there is none or little reciprocation. It is heart shattering. In fact, many have given up on love, many have hardened their hearts because of the brokenness that has left them wounded, disillusioned and devastated from pouring into a one-sided relationship.

The other word used for love is **Racham**, a love that is complete.

"Peter turned and saw the disciple whom Jesus loved following them; the one who also had

**leaned back on His chest at the supper and had
said, "Lord, who is it that is going to betray
You?"** (John 21:20)

This is an example of the Apostle John, who loved
Jesus as Jesus loved Him. John openly expressed His
love for our Lord as he laid his head upon the chest
of Jesus. This type of love and tenderness that is
returned is the **Racham**. This returned love speaks
of our commitment to the *Bridegroom*. The new
covenant is established on a love relationship
where our obedience is not out of fear, duty, guilt,
shame or condemnation, but solely and
wholeheartedly, motivated from a heart of love. It
is all about the heart.

Exposing the god of perception

Marriage is a covenant set up by God. Throughout
scripture and within our daily lives, our TRIUNE
GOD has repeatedly revealed to us that His

intention is to bring us to a place of faith and trust in an immutable God who loves us individually and corporately, infinitely. His ultimate goal is to captivate our hearts with His love so that we can spontaneously release our hearts to be all that He says we are. Unfortunately, because of the lies we have believed about the Father, Son and Holy Ghost, it prevents us from wholeheartedly releasing ourselves in faith. Lies prevent us from having the right perspective towards our God, resulting in our experience of spiritual death. There are many believers who see God in the Old Testament as harsh, a dictator, a judge and see the God of the New Testament as loving, kind and tender. In this book, we will see that our God, Saviour, Redeemer, Bridegroom from the beginning has been relentlessly pursuing us for bridal intimacy as He draws us to Himself as a bride. Every product knows that only the manufacturer knows the product in detail. Only our Manufacturer can change our hearts towards Him as He transforms our lives. He does this by repeatedly revealing His Heart for you and me through revelation of His written Word and through His daily whispers to our hearts. As He does, He melts our walls of defences and captivates our hearts propelling us to live according to His original intention with greater commitment from a heart level and by greater revelatory knowledge. You cannot demand commitment and get it. COMMITMENT is the by-product of an awakening.

During this time of being at loggerheads with my estranged husband, I was sent a text by him to inquire if I were at home because he wanted to come by. When I read the text, I interpreted the text as he wanted to come around but not whilst I was at home. That evening when he came by, we spoke and I realised that my assumption/

interpretation of the text he had sent was not only wrong, but it revealed some of the wounds I was carrying in my heart. It gave me the wrong impression of my husband's intention whilst deceiving me in the process. It was eye opening because I began to realise that WE INTERPRET BY THE STATE OF OUR HEARTS. That is, if our hearts are wounded, our interpretation will be twisted. If our hearts are whole, we are more likely to be objective in our interpretation. Proverbs 4:23 in the NLT version of the Bible says it this way:

"Guard your heart above all else, for it determines the course of your life."

This scripture reminds me that if I had acted on my presumption that day when I received the text, I would have reacted defensively and most likely attacked my husband with my words. You see my interpretation of his text would have determined the course of my action.

This sobered me, so much so, I began to see how easily we can be deceived by our heart when we are not dealing with its issues. These seek to dictate attitudes and actions to us when we are not surrendering our pain to our Father in Heaven. Jeremiah 17:9 (AMP) says it this way:

> *"The heart is deceitful above all things and it is extremely sick; Who can understand it fully and know its secret motives?"*

WOW! It made me begin to look at what other lies I had believed because of the state of my heart. What other things had I heard that I interpreted wrongly because my heart was deceived? What scriptures did I read that I misconstrued because my heart was deceived?

Many of us are divided about the character and nature of our God. Many will still tell you that, in the Old Testament, God was wicked, demanding, harsh with believing that, in the New Testament, He is loving, merciful and kind. Yet the Bible says in Hebrews 13:8:

> *"Jesus Christ is [eternally changeless, always] the same yesterday and today and forever."*

If God never changes, then what is feeding our minds and our hearts of this ludicrous contrast in nature?

I believe what has given us a twisted view of our God is the law-based religion we have been fed and partaken of for centuries. We have been brainwashed to think a certain way. We see that one of the obstacles Jesus had on earth when He taught was religious thinkers that opposed His teaching because they were taught an eye for an eye, a tooth for a tooth. Although Jesus came to change this thinking by His teachings, today we still have the same problem with religious thinking.

In Matthew 5 the chapter begins with Jesus outlining the attitudes of Kingdom that we should have like:

> *"Blessed [spiritually prosperous, happy, to be admired] are the poor in spirit [those devoid of spiritual arrogance, those who regard themselves as insignificant], for theirs is the kingdom of heaven [both now and forever]."*

Further in that passage He begins to reveal our identity as the people of God.

> *"You are the salt of the earth; but if the salt has lost its taste (purpose), how can it be made*

salty? It is no longer good for anything, but to be thrown out and walked on by people [when the walkways are wet and slippery]."

But then He mentions in verse 17:

"Do not think that I came to do away with or undo the Law [of Moses] or the [writings of the] Prophets; I did not come to destroy but to fulfill."

As a teacher who taught in schools for almost two decades, and as a parent, I have given many different forms of punishment in my time. Over time, I have realised that the punishment may change the behaviour but the heart does not always change resulting in, behaviour modification. The reason the behaviour changes is because of the spirit of fear that is released through punishment and the spirit of intimidation that is released through threats. The heart does not change because, only God changes hearts through awakening us; He does not use fear of any kind to inspire change. However, when motivated by fear it causes the heart to become emotionally detached out of which leads to a wrong perception of the Heart of God. Truthfully, we cannot experience a heart to Heart connection with God whilst having a twisted view of God towards us. However, when we truly see the Heart of God towards us, it melts our own hearts removing the deception that prevented us seeing clearly. So you see, what we believe about God will determine the depth of the intimacy we will experience in our relationship with Him and as direct result, how we represent Him to others by our treatment. He cares more about our heart and its response than any robotic action of fear. You see bridal intimacy starts with a heart to Heart connection. Unfortunately, we have been so immersed in law-based teaching, that we have learnt how to exist without any Heart to heart connection or response. That is, we obey the law, but our hearts are far from Him. This is not a heart that is motivated by His love, instead, motivated by fear and trepidation. Jesus came to show us who we truly are. By embracing His truth, we are embracing our real selves; thus, a change of perception transforms our heart and fulfils the law.

In John 8 we see an example of an adulterous woman who would have been stoned by a group of "good-hearted" religious Jews intent on obeying the law. The law that stipulates that if a man or woman was adulterous, they were to be put to death (Leviticus 20:10). Jesus, the Righteous One, the pure Lamb of God, the propitiation of all our sins, came and, for the first time in history, these men were challenged to look, think, move from their hearts not to robotically regurgitate the law.

Jesus said, *"He who is without [any] sin among you, let him be the first to throw a stone at her."* (John 8:7)

His very words challenged the men to look at their own hearts and, for the first time I believe, they had to consider their own failings and were forced to acknowledge that they were not without sin and so could not throw the stone. Jesus was displaying how mercy triumphs over judgment. As Jesus bent down to the ground and wrote in the sand with His finger, the Pharisees who heard Him *stood still for a few moments and then* began to leave slowly, one by one, beginning with the older men. Eventually only Jesus and the woman remained, and Jesus looked up.

Jesus: *Dear* woman, where is everyone? *Are we*

alone? Did no one step forward to condemn you?

Woman Caught in Adultery: Lord, no one *has condemned me.*

Jesus: *I do not condemn you either. Go. From now on, sin no more.*

I believe this woman went away and was forever changed from this encounter. She experienced the mercy and love of God that led her to repentance. She encountered the heart of God for her and all the while experienced His love over the law. Today, the Lord wants to show us His heart for us. When our hearts are captivated by His love for us, we not only fulfil the law, but we are forever changed in our hearts. Jesus captivated this woman's heart by dealing with the WHYS of her issues. *Her heart was crying out for love.* Jesus extended the purest form of love to her. I believe she was able to repent that day from the heart because of the love, the grace, the mercy she was shown by Jesus. Throughout scripture we will see that our God has always loved us and has foreseen what we will need and has provided accordingly as He continues to pursue us. He is always seeking out our hearts to trust Him more as He reveals His heart for us again and again. It is important for us to note that true change of heart comes when we encounter the Father's heart, our Bridegroom's heart towards us FIRST, then our hearts fall in line. The awakening is initiated by Him from the foundation of the world, as He pursues us for a heart response.

Cultivating Bridal Intimacy

What wrong perceptions of the Godhead are driving you?

*

What law are you upholding rather than dealing with the heart of the matter?

*

What does your Bridegroom, Jesus, reveal to you about His heart for you?

*

Heart change can only be made by our Creator.
He does not threaten us for this change, He loves us into this change.

Chapter 2

AWAKENING TO HIS COMMITMENT

"No other gods"

"I cannot be substituted. I am your living source."

- GOD

Throughout the Bible, and most importantly, throughout our lives, we see God's perusal of our hearts. Yet though we have read His commandments to us, we have most times interpreted them as do's and don'ts rather than understanding from His heart to our hearts; the Father's Heart, the Heart of our Bridegroom behind these life transforming statements.

These commandments, given to Moses for His people, tell us about His commitment, His vows to us which are His **'ketubah'** to us or the marriage contract. It outlines the expectation of our Bridegroom and for us to be one with His proposal to us. However, throughout scripture God has never asked us to do something He Himself has not already done. He will also not ask you to do something He has not empowered you to do. The first one is, "YOU SHALL HAVE NO OTHER GODS BUT ME". Do you think that is a reasonable statement? Would you like your spouse to have a secret lover while he/she claims to be committed to you? I am sure if you are thinking with the right heart you would say undoubtedly, NO! Yet, we expect God to accept our half-hearted attempts to build with Him while we flirt with all other diversions...

This first commandment speaks volumes of our Father, the Son and Holy Spirit's commitment to us. God is saying I am committed to you first and foremost. You are My most treasured possession. All I do is because of My commitment to you. You are My first priority. There is no other in creation that I have made My priority like you. We see examples of this truth throughout scripture.

> *Then God said, "Let Us (Father, Son, Holy Spirit)*
> *make man in Our image, according to Our*
> *likeness [not physical, but a spiritual personality*
> *and moral likeness]; and let them have*
> *complete authority over the fish of the sea, the*

> **birds of the air, the cattle, and over the entire earth, and over everything that creeps and crawls on the earth."** (Genesis 1:26)

We are the only created beings made in the image of God, the Three in One, having body, soul and spirit. We are also assigned rulership and authority over all creation.

> **"For you are a holy people [set apart] to the Lord your God; the Lord your God has chosen you out of all the peoples on the face of the earth to be a people for His own possession [that is, His very special treasure]."** (Deuteronomy 7:6)

We see that we are the only created being that He has separated unto Himself, set apart as His own people but also as Holy. Deuteronomy 14:2 reiterates this truth:

"For you are a holy people to the LORD your God, and the LORD has chosen you to be a people for His own possession out of all the peoples who are on the face of the earth."

Matthew 10:29-31 reveals our value to our God. It says:

"Are not two little sparrows sold for a copper coin? And yet not one of them falls to the ground apart from your Father's will. But even the very hairs of your head are all numbered [for the Father is sovereign and has complete knowledge]. So do not fear; you are more valuable than many sparrows."

It is clear that we are invaluable, and we have been put in a class of our own. As He watches over us, He even knows the amount of hairs on our head. Our hair sheds daily and yet the Creator of the universe and everything in it, knows the updated number of hairs on every head all the time. INCREDIBLE! So one could say that, undoubtedly, our Father in Heaven has made us HIS MAIN PRIORITY demonstrating His commitment to us, His faithfulness, His trustworthiness, His immutability. As a married woman who has felt the pains of infidelity, our God is telling us undoubtedly that He is fully committed to us. This is why He could ask us, as we think about our vows to Him as a Bridegroom, to ensure we have NO OTHER gods.

When we question whether we are being faithful to God, we naturally think we are faithful. However, when we perceive God as an afterthought, a side kick, a backup plan, is that faithfulness? Entertaining other gods is easier than we think. Recently, I was looking at the appearance of our ministry account depleted of finances. As I spoke to our Father in Heaven, I reminded Him of a new course I would be doing for the institute and asked if I could get a specific number of students in order to pay the bills and build up the depleted funds. In my heart, I heard the Father say, He is the only Source and the institute is one of the ways He could bless me, but He has numerous ways. He said if my faith is in the resource (the "institute") He has given me, then I have made it into a source (god) in my life. I realised that when we look to or depend on a resource as a source, we are creating an idol in our life. I was conversing with the Creator who has a plethora of ways to bless me; yet, I was choosing to limit Him by looking to one resource when I should only be looking to the SOURCE of all resources.

"When you were my young bride, you loved me and followed me through the barren desert. You belonged to me alone, like the first part of the harvest, and I severely punished those who

mistreated you." (Jeremiah 2:2-3)

Idolatry can be defined as anything we seek to put before God Himself. As I shared above, this is easily done by us when we fail to trust the heart of our Father, Bridegroom, Comforter wholeheartedly. Our failure to trust is not based on His failings but on our own failings. I have come to realise that when we judge our circumstances from our own eyes it warps our perception, which in turn indoctrinates us to work harder to change our circumstance, rather than fix our eyes on Jesus or to consciously look through His eyes being aware of His heart towards you and me. Scripture is clear, *you shall not make for yourself any idol, nor bow down to it or worship it.* Another way of saying this is do not treat God as a substitute or a sidekick.

"You, my people, have sinned in two ways—you have rejected me, the source of life-giving water, and you've tried to collect water in cracked and leaking pits dug in the ground." (Jeremiah 2:13)

There are two Lords/lords, our Lord Jesus and the spirt of Mammon. Both are asking us to be led by them. They are both fighting for our attention. Yet, our Bridegroom has asked us to fix our eyes on Him alone. The spirit of Mammon wants us to see value based on how much we are benefiting or gaining monetarily rather than to live a life of faith in the One True God.

Cultivating Bridal intimacy

What causes someone to be unfaithful?

*

In what areas of your relationship with God have you failed to trust Him?

*

What forms of neglect have you shown to your Bridegroom?

*

Fix your eyes on His unwavering commitment to you and allow it to manifest in you with greater or deeper commitment.

Chapter 3

AWAKENING HIS IDENTITY IN YOU

"You shall not misuse My name"

*"My name is a weapon in your mouth. Use it with
the honour in which I gave you."*

- BRIDEGROOM

What is in a name? What is the purpose of a name? Everything and every place, every animal and every person has a name. A name reveals the nature and character and the purpose of the thing or the person. A chair by its very name implies its function. By your very name, I too believe God by design, has hidden your purpose within the meaning of your name. When someone calls your name, your purpose is being prophesied and it goes forth to open and close doors, ordering your steps according to His plans and purposes for you.

My name is Christine Annmarie Nelson. Christine means *follower of Christ*, anointed one, Messiah. Annmarie means *grace* and *bitterness*. Nelson means *champion*. I told the Lord I did not like the meaning of Marie because it means bitterness; a negative meaning, I thought. He told me that He would use me to take away the bitterness of others as I am being awakened to His continuous forgiveness towards me. Essentially, the meaning of my name implies that I am purposed by PAPA God to paint, smear and anoint others to be the kings and priests they are by His grace as sins of the heart are dealt with so they can walk as champions. Sounds like an overcomer or how the Apostle Paul puts it, "more than a conqueror." This is not unique to me. I believe this is true of us all: we are God's workmanship sent to bring Him glory and our very purpose and identity is hidden in what we are called. This is why throughout scripture we will notice that when the Lord speaks to and about us, He only speaks LIFE. He says we are "the apple of His eye", we are His "treasured possession" and much more. So see, by what He calls you and me, it speaks of our identity in Him because all that He is so are we.

Religion has presented the name of our Lord Jesus as a lucky charm to be added to the end of prayer and, in some circles of the world, His name is used as a curse word. Religion and the world have undermined the power in the name causing it to be impotent. Yet, I believe we completely misunderstood the scriptures that encourage us to, 'do it in the name of Jesus.' This concept of doing things in His name, reveals the authority in the name of Jesus, but it also implies *we are in* the NAME Jesus. Because we are in His name, we can rest in the authority the name carries. The awakening to His many names reveals to us the aspects of His nature and character of which we are blessed to be the dwelling place.

I believe, as believers in Christ, being given His name is not just a privilege but it speaks of the name change that a bride undergoes in marriage. The name change implies a change of identity because of who you are now consciously aware that you are connected to. There is also a weighty presence or glory when the name is said because of the relational bond with the person. The name also speaks of authority and a new status; the name speaks of the power of attorney as inheritors. There are many scriptures of the privilege we have been given as His offspring, carriers of His Name. This implies that since we are *in* Christ, all that He is we are too. If He is the Light so are we. When we enter a dark place, our light emanates. It was not added to us, but we were immersed in Him and were created in the same image, sewn from the same cloth, so to speak; bone of His Bone and flesh of His Flesh.

When we understand the privilege and the responsibility of being given the name of Christ (Anointed One), we will be mindful of how we use His name. So many times, we can use the Lord's name in vain by using His name to imply that we are speaking on behalf of Him (God) or we are being His representative to add weight to what we are saying in order to manipulate or control others. This responsibility of carrying His name, requires us to be conscious of the Spirit of the Fear of the Lord in order to not misuse His name. This is why scripture encourages us to let our yes be yes and our no be no. The Bible also says not to swear or make a vow. Keep our language simple yet, truthful.

We can only reflect His name as we have experienced Him in that facet of Himself. Jesus, our Bridegroom, reveals Himself through many names. He is your Advocate, the One that has you covered. He endorses you because when He sees you, He sees Himself.

"My dear children, I write this to you so that you will not sin. But if anybody does sin, we

have an advocate with the Father--Jesus Christ, the Righteous One." (1 John 2:1)

Another name He has, is the Author and Perfecter of our Faith, which means He is the beginning of our real life and He is also the One who has perfected what He has begun. So, it is not up to our self-will or our might, but He is the Perfecter of our faith. We can be confident that what He has authored or engineered, created in you, He has ensured it is perfected or is completed.

"Fixing our eyes on Jesus, the author and perfecter of faith, who for the joy set before Him endured the cross, despising the shame, and has sat down at the right hand of the throne of God." (Hebrews 12:2)

His name is Faithful and True. The fact that faithful and true are in the same line suggests to me they are one of the same. A person who is true is faithful and a person who is faithful is true. Someone who is faithful is committed, devoted, loyal, dedicated. Wow! Every person I know wants a spouse who replicates these qualities. Why? Because Faithfulness is in us.

> *"I saw heaven standing open and there before me was a white horse, whose rider is called Faithful and True. With justice he judges and wages war."* **(Revelation 19:11)**

Your Bridegroom is your I AM.

> *"Jesus said to them, "Truly, truly, I say to you, before Abraham was, I am."* **(John 8:58)**

He is your PRESENT. This name of Jesus cautions us to not look too far ahead nor to dwell on the past because He is our I AM. When we are in our future, we don't have the grace, so we are anxious and worried. When we immerse ourselves in our past it keeps us hopeless. We are carriers of the I AM, our Bridegroom, Who is our Present Help.

When we are awakened to His names we walk in the oneness of His names as we manifest the authority, the meaning, the purpose of those names. The Bible uses the word 'name' in many scriptures as the examples below:

> *A good name [earned by honourable behaviour, godly wisdom, moral courage, and personal integrity] is more desirable than great riches; And favour is better than silver and gold.* **(Proverbs 22:1)**

A name reveals the character and nature of a person.

Then those who feared the Lord [with awe-filled reverence] spoke to one another; and the Lord paid attention and heard it, and a book of remembrance was written before Him of those who fear the Lord [with an attitude of reverence and respect] and who esteem His name. **(Malachi 3:16)**

A name carries the Spirit of the Fear of the Lord to walk in awe and reverence.

For "whoever calls on the name of the Lord [in prayer] will be saved." **(Romans 10:13)**

There is salvation in His name.

"Pray, then in this way: 'Our Father, who is in heaven, Hallowed be Your name." **(Matthew 6:9)**

There is authority in His name.

> *"...so that at the name of Jesus every knee shall bow [in submission], of those who are in heaven and on earth, [11] and that every tongue will confess and openly acknowledge that Jesus Christ is Lord (sovereign God), to the glory of God the Father."* **(Philippians 2:10-11)**

There is reverence in His name.

> *And there is salvation in no one else; for there is no other name under heaven that has been given among people by which we must be saved [for God has provided the world no alternative for salvation]."* **(Acts 4:12)**

There is power in His name.

> *"Therefore," [says the Lord] "behold, I will make them know—This time I will make them know My power and My might; And they will know and recognize [without any doubt] that My Name is the Lord."* (Jeremiah 16:21)

So we see there is redemptive purpose in His name, there is consequence to the use of His name. Back to our original question – *What is in a name?* Purpose, consequences, authority, identity, inheritance, power, salvation, reverential fear, destiny, promotion - all are in a name. Jesus reveals His confidence in Himself through you that you cannot misuse His name when His names are awakened in you. You can only live out or emanate the truth in His names. You see, He reveals His names to you so you can live out the reality of Who He is *in you*.

Cultivating Bridal Intimacy

What is your name?

*

Do you embrace the truth that as the Bride of Christ you carry His name and the nature and character of what His name reveals?

*

Are you representing the truth of His name?

*

REMEMBER:

You manifest the truth of His names as you are awakened to them. The awakening prevents us from misusing it because His name reveals His person.

Chapter 4

AWAKENING YOU TO HIS DESIRE TO BE WITH YOU

"Keep the Sabbath holy"

"The awakened enter My rest

because they believe."

- BRIDEGROOM

"Remember the Sabbath day by keeping it holy. Six days you shall labour and do all your work, but the seventh day is a sabbath to the Lord your God. On it you shall not do any work, neither you, nor your son or daughter, nor your male or female servant, nor your animals, nor any foreigner residing in your towns. For in six days the Lord made the heavens and the earth, the sea, and all that is in them, but he rested on the seventh day. Therefore the Lord blessed the Sabbath day and made it holy." (Exodus 20:8-11)

When I hear this instruction of the Sabbath, I hear the Bridegroom inquiring, beckoning, inviting us if you will, saying, "Would you give Me a date day where I can restore your perspective and your heart?"

So what is the Sabbath? It is a day for you to sit with the Lover of your soul and tell all, sharing your hurts, your joys, your questions, your concerns, your passions; and expecting Him to reveal to you His perspective and His heart which bring restoration, healing, direction and ability to walk in freedom.

To practice the Sabbath challenges us to grow in our trust of our Father to provide for us when we do not work. Too often we get into the mode of strife or works without realising that we are not being led by the Spirit of God; instead, we are being driven by the arm of the flesh. Practicing the Sabbath realigns us and draws us back into the arms of our Bridegroom, His arms of refuge, His arms of security, His arms of peace; albeit silencing the voice of strife. This voice has ways of deceiving us so much so that we are convinced we are being led by the Spirit, but we are really being driven by results, recognition, approval of men, ultimately selfish ambition. Entering His rest and making it our dwelling place prevents us from falling into the pitfalls of twisted motives which take us off course whilst hardening our hearts. Hebrews 4 describes the promise of entering this realm of rest whilst giving us more insight:

> *Therefore, since a promise remains of entering His rest, let us fear lest any of you seem to have come short of it. For indeed the gospel was preached to us as well as to them; but the word which they heard did not profit them, not being mixed with faith in those who heard it. For we who have believed do enter that rest, as He has said: "So I swore in My wrath, 'They shall not enter My rest,' although the works were finished from the foundation of the world. For He has spoken in a certain place of the*

seventh day in this way: "And God rested on the seventh day from all His works"; and again in this place: "They shall not enter My rest." Since therefore it remains that some must enter it, and those to whom it was first preached did not enter because of disobedience, again He designates a certain day, saying in David, "Today," after such a long time, as it has been said: "Today, if you will hear His voice, Do not harden your hearts." For if Joshua had given them rest, then He would not afterward have spoken of another day. [9] There remains therefore a rest for the people of God. For he who has entered His rest has himself also ceased from his works as God did from His. (Hebrews 4:1-10)

We see that this scripture is a fulfilment of the command given to us in the Old Testament. I describe it as a fulfilment because it describes and outlines the implications of entering the rest. First of all, we see that those who enter this rest are those who *believe*, reiterating the importance of trusting His word to us. Again, my experience of this word tells me that, when we receive His word with faith and not just with our intellect, we are shifted into a place of rest. As a Minister of His word, one of the most heart wrenching things I sometimes see when teaching or when receiving teaching, is an arrogant display of how we receive His word; more times received as intellectual knowledge rather than life transforming revelation. I see this attitude with my teenager when I speak, sometimes it is as if, even before I speak, he has this look like he has tuned me out because he already knows. This is frightening to me when I see it in me, in those to whom I minister, or in my son because truth and facts are not the same. The attitude we have in receiving truth must be different to the attitude we have in receiving facts. Facts are subjected to change. Truth is truth no matter what! It is eternal. By its eternal implications, truth should get our attention and we should be open for it to set us free because that is the only reason why truth is sent. True freedom relinquishes all that restricts us. We must believe Him at His WORD in order to enter His rest, His freedom.

In addition, we see that the labour or the works had been finished before the foundation of the world indicating to us that our job NOW is not to labour, but to believe in what is already so in order to bring forth the manifestation. Our work today as believers is to believe in the finished work of Christ. Failure to believe causes our hearts to be hardened. Essentially, we see that proof we have entered this rest is that we have ceased from works.

Today, if you hear His voice, "Turn off your phone,

turn off the radio, turn off the television, silence all the distractions as I the Lover of your soul desire your undivided attention." Will you be too preoccupied to hear and obey? Will you just BE with the Lover of your soul? Will you express freely your frustrations, the impotence of your works and just be? Allow Him to remind you how adequate you already are, how fearfully and wonderfully He made you, how more than a conqueror you are, how ONE you are with Him. Then everything you feel incapable of, you will quickly realise you are capable because you already carry a limitless supply of His ability. **It is in this place of rest that you hear these affirmations that keep you soaring.**

My previous paragraph is my deliberate attempt to demonstrate to you that Jesus is the Lord of the Sabbath. This is why He should be able to ask you to just be with Him and you will not allow work, chores, your anxious thoughts or the busyness of life to cause you to silence His voice in you. The Sabbath is not supposed to control you, it is subjected to you. Jesus had many instances throughout scripture where the religious leaders of the day were enraged by the casual way He seemed to overlook this sacred day the Pharisees considered the Sabbath. Here is an example in Matthew 12:1-14:

> *"At that time Jesus went through the grain fields on the Sabbath. And His disciples were hungry, and began to pluck heads of grain and to eat. And when the Pharisees saw it, they said to Him, "Look, Your disciples are doing what is not lawful to do on the Sabbath!" But He said to them, "Have you not read what David did when he was hungry, he and those who were with him: how he entered the house of God and ate the showbread which was not lawful for*

him to eat, nor for those who were with him, but only for the priests? Or have you not read in the law that on the Sabbath the priests in the temple profane the Sabbath, and are blameless? Yet I say to you that in this place there is One greater than the temple. But if you had known what this means, 'I desire mercy and not sacrifice,' you would not have condemned the guiltless. For the Son of Man is Lord even of the Sabbath." Now when He had departed from there, He went into their synagogue. And behold, there was a man who had a withered hand. And they asked Him, saying, "Is it lawful to heal on the Sabbath?"—that they might accuse Him. Then He said to them, "What man is there among you who has one sheep, and if it falls into a pit on the Sabbath, will not lay hold of it and lift it out? Of how much more value then is a man than a sheep? Therefore it is lawful to do good on the Sabbath." Then He said to the man, "Stretch out your hand." And

he stretched it out, and it was restored as whole as the other. Then the Pharisees went out and plotted against Him, how they might destroy Him."

Don't you just love Jesus?! My goodness! He is LORD OF THE SABBATH! Jesus made a point of demonstrating to the Pharisees that David, when he was hungry, ate the showbread from the house of God though it was unlawful for him to eat. He mentioned that in the law the priests in the temple profane the Sabbath yet were considered blameless, then unveiled Himself as GREATER than the temple. However, because their eyes were veiled, they were unable to acknowledge Him and did not get His point. They then tried to set Him up or to get Him to put His foot in His mouth and Jesus gave this analogy. He said if a man has one sheep and it fell into a pit on the Sabbath, will he not lift it out? Is a sheep more valuable than a man? He then demonstrated and fulfilled this wonderful commandment at the same time by COMPLETELY RESTORING the hand of the man with the withered hand. If you missed His announcement, Jesus was saying, "THE SABBATH DOES NOT CONTROL YOU, IT IS SUBJECTED TO YOU. EVERYDAY, INCLUDING THE SABBATH, IS A SACRED DAY THAT YOU SHOW MERCY BECAUSE THAT IS WHAT I DESIRE." Will you be an expression of mercy (compassion or forgiveness shown towards someone whom it is within one's power to punish or harm) not sacrifice (an act of slaughtering an animal or person or surrendering a possession as an offering to God)? The Lover of your soul is the Lord of the Sabbath. He wants you to see every day as sacred, to show mercy and to set aside quality time for Him to restore you and heal your soul. Happy Sabbath as you immerse yourself in greater levels of intimacy. Come bride, come to this place of rest, a place of being - not doing, a place of belonging and a place of believing and conscious union in His presence.

Cultivating Bridal intimacy

What works are you still trying to accomplish when it is already finished before the foundation of the world?

*

What doubts are you still battling that are causing you to labour?

*

Is the Sabbath dictating to you rather than being subjected to you?

*

Will you make room for the Lover of your Soul?

*

When you believe it is already finished you never have to become nor work towards, you just need to remind yourself Who finished it... Whose you are... Then call it forth.

Chapter 5

AWAKENING HIS PATTERN TO YOU AS YOUR DAD AND MUM

"Honour thy father and mother"

"When you can honour your father and mother, you can honour Me and cleave to Me as Your Bridegroom."

- PROPHETIC UTTERANCE

Your parents are a shadow of My role in your life as ABBA (Father) and EL SHADDAI (The Breastie One).

What is the role of a dad? To protect (SAFE PLACE) and to provide (SOURCE-CENTRAL for your emotional wellbeing), these anchor a child in security. Dads are most time viewed as the disciplinarians. Dads provide stability in a home.

What is the role of a mum? To nurture you so that you can give birth to your destiny, to teach you how to be faithful, to be tenacious. Her aim is to cultivate a place where you are valued, you feel safe and secure.

1 John 4:20 lays a principle of how you treat what you see as an indication of how you treat the unseen. It says:

"If anyone says, 'I love God,' and hates (works against) his [Christian] brother he is a liar; for the one who does not love his brother whom he has seen, cannot love God whom he has not seen."

We see Jesus apply the same principle in another demonstration in Matthew 25:34-40:

"Then the King will say to those on His right hand, 'Come, you blessed of My Father, inherit the kingdom prepared for you from the foundation of the world: for I was hungry and you gave Me food; I was thirsty and you gave Me drink; I was a stranger and you took Me in; I was naked and you clothed Me; I was sick and you visited Me; I was in prison and you came to Me'." "Then the righteous will answer Him, saying, 'Lord, when did we see You hungry and feed You, or thirsty and give You drink? When did we see You a stranger and take You in, or

naked and clothe You? Or when did we see You sick, or in prison, and come to You?' And the King will answer and say to them, 'Assuredly, I say to you, inasmuch as you did it to one of the least of these My brethren, you did it to Me'."

Jesus is again saying what you do for the visible you are doing for the invisible. *So honour your parents for, as you honour them, you are honouring Me.* I believe with Jesus as our Bridegroom, we get to experience God the Father through Him and God El Shaddai - the Breastie One - through Him as we partake of God with us in our Bridegroom.

When we look at the word *honour* as used in Exodus 20:12, the Hebrew language defines it as feeding parents, clothing parents, and helping them come in and out. This is certainly not a definition we have associated with the word honour; naturally this sounds more like the definition of being charitable. The Hebrew word is Kavod which is really a poor translation because the true meaning of Kavod is dignity. When we keep our parents clothed and fed when they can no longer do this for themselves, this is a preservation of their dignity. Another word for honour is Morah which means to not sit in someone else's seat or not to interrupt. This speaks of us being selfless enough to allow someone to go first whether that be giving up our seat or allowing them to speak without interruption. This sounds like a reiteration of Philippians 2:4:

> ***Do not merely look out for your own personal interests, but also for the interests of others.***

How does the Bible describe or define the word honour? Most times we have a limited perspective of its meaning as respecting or putting others above yourself. Throughout scripture we see these meanings and much more.

The Bible tells a story about Noah, a man that scripture describes to have stood out among all men in his time as a godly man. So much so, he was mandated by God to warn the people of the impending end of the world as they knew it and how to prevent themselves from the same fate. The Bible outlines how, after this traumatic ordeal, the entire world was destroyed leaving the eight people who were in the ark, Noah and his family members. We are not told how this impacted Noah, but the Bible outlines what happened after this calamity.

> *"Then God spoke to Noah and to his sons with him, saying, 'Now behold, I Myself do establish My covenant with you, and with your descendants after you; and with every*

living creature that is with you, the birds, the cattle, and every beast of the earth with you; of all that comes out of the ark, even every beast of the earth. I establish My covenant with you; and all flesh shall never again be cut off by the water of the flood, neither shall there again be a flood to destroy the earth.' God said, 'This is the sign of the covenant which I am making between Me and you and every living creature that is with you, for all successive generations; I set My bow in the cloud, and it shall be for a sign of a covenant between Me and the earth. It shall come about, when I bring a cloud over the earth, that the bow will be seen in the cloud, and I will remember My covenant, which is between Me and you and every living creature of all flesh; and never again shall the water become a flood to destroy all flesh. When the bow is in the cloud, then I will look upon it, to remember the everlasting covenant between God and every living creature of all flesh that is on the earth.' And God said to Noah, 'This is the sign of the covenant which I have established between Me and all flesh that is on the earth.' Now the sons of Noah who came out of the ark were Shem and Ham and Japheth; and Ham was the father of Canaan.

The sons of Noah who came out of the ark were Shem and Ham and Japheth. Ham would become the father of Canaan.

These three were the sons of Noah, and from these the whole earth was populated. Then Noah began farming and planted a vineyard. He drank of the wine and became drunk, and uncovered himself inside his tent. Ham, the father of Canaan, saw the nakedness of his father, and told his two brothers outside. But Shem and Japheth took a garment and laid it upon both their shoulders and walked backward and covered the nakedness of their father; and their faces were turned away, so that they did not see their father's nakedness. When Noah awoke from his wine, he knew what his youngest son had done to him. So he said, "Cursed be Canaan; A servant of servants He shall be to his brothers." He also said, "Blessed be the Lord, The God of Shem; And let Canaan be his servant. "May God enlarge Japheth, And let him dwell in the tents of Shem; And let Canaan be his servant." Noah lived three hundred and fifty years after the flood. So all the days of Noah were nine hundred and fifty years, and he died." (Genesis 9:8-29)

So we see that God gathered around all eight

survivors and made a covenant with them and blessed them. We see that after the blessing, Noah began farming and he grew grapes which he made wine from and drank until he became drunk. The Bible describes Noah as naked when his son Ham found him and went and told his brothers. This angered Noah and, due to spiritual amnesia, Noah forgot that the God of the Heavens and the Earth had already blessed his sons and His Word is final. Noah went on to curse his son Ham for not honouring him by not preserving his *dignity* because Ham exposed Noah's shame. The other two sons honoured their father by covering his weakness so to speak. This reminds me of the scripture that says:

"Love covers a multitude of sin." (1 Peter 4:8).

So, we see that the word honour is defined scripturally as "to cover".

We see that there was a curse that followed this dishonour to not just Ham, the father of Canaan, but it went on to affect the entire people of Canaan. This curse of Noah was so believed over the blessings of God that it affected generations after Ham. Noah cursed Ham and his sons to be servants of servants, slaves really! When we dishonour our parents publicly before our children, we are causing them to continue the trait of dishonour (children often do what you do rather that listen to what you say). We see that when we dishonour, we can either be instilling in our children's children to be a generation of slaves or a generation of free men. Yet I believe, if the words of God had been believed over the words of Noah, that generation would not have lived in condemnation but in the blessing that was given to them by God Himself. God's words trump all other words. This is not to say dishonour is right, but I want to ensure scripture is presented in a balanced way. When we do wrong, we do not have to suffer in condemnation forever and ever. Our Bridegroom Jesus came and ensured we were justified which means in His eyes we are innocent, justified - just as if we have never sinned. By aligning our thoughts and our perception with His, we are setting our minds on things above.

Ultimately, it is imperative we understand there is a call to honour, to dignify, to cover, to not sit in someone else's seat, and to honour our parents because as we do to them who are visible, we are doing to God who is invisible.

Cultivating Bridal Intimacy

Are you experiencing our Bridegroom's honour of you?

*

How does He dignify you?

*

How does He cover your dignity?

*

How are you honouring Him in your life?

*

Write down the ways in which He honours you and allow your heart to fall in love with Him over and over again.

Chapter 6

AWAKENING TO HIS POWER OF LOVE IN YOU

"Do not kill"

"As the lover of your soul I will rejuvenate you,
revitalize you, invigorate you,
never causing you harm."

- JESUS (PROPHETIC UTTERANCE)

"Thou shalt not kill - Embrace how I have loved

you treated you and be likewise so that no resentment, bitterness, slander, gossip can be found in you. "You have heard that the ancients were told, 'You shall not commit murder' and 'Whoever commits murder shall be liable to the court.' But I say to you that everyone who is angry with his brother shall be guilty before the court; and whoever says to his brother, 'You good-for-nothing,' shall be guilty before the supreme court; and whoever says, 'You fool,' shall be guilty enough to go into the fiery hell. Therefore if you are presenting your offering at the altar, and there remember that your brother has something against you, leave your offering there before the altar and go; first be reconciled to your brother, and then come and present your offering. Make friends quickly with your opponent at law while you are with him on the way, so that your opponent may not hand you over to the judge, and the judge to the officer, and you be thrown into prison." (Matthew 5:21-25)

When reading this passage of scripture, we see Jesus describing a deeper level of this notion "to kill". He is not purporting the ultimate of putting a knife to someone or a gun and taking a life, though these are forms of killing. He points out ways in which we kill that are different from what I described above. He describes killing through resentment, bitterness, slander, gossip and anger. If we look closely at these words, we will see that all these manifestations are birthed from the seed of unforgiveness which is an indication of our limited perception of how we have been wronged.

Joseph is a good example of someone who had incredibly difficult circumstances so that incurring a murderous heart would have been considered justifiable. The Bible describes Joseph as a teenager (young man) who had a series of dreams. In his dream he saw himself above his brothers. He shared his dream, whether out of pride or excitement, with those closest to him, his family. His brothers were so angry about the favouritism he was shown already by their father, that, when he shared his dreams, they thought there is no way this is going to happen. They instinctively dug a hole and left him in there. Soon the plot thickens as they sold their brother to some merchants passing by. Joseph was then bought by the house of Pharaoh. The wife of Pharaoh thought she could have her way with Joseph and, when he refused her sexual advances, she accused him of sexual harassment. Joseph was then thrown into prison by Pharaoh. In prison he met two other men who had dreams, and with the help of God, he interpreted their dreams. One of the men promised that, when he got out, he would tell them about Joseph so he could be free but, alas, Joseph was forgotten in prison. In all of this God was working everything out for Joseph to fulfil the dream he dreamt years before. Soon Pharaoh had a dream and needed help in interpreting it. One of the young men from the prison he had helped with his dream before, remembered Joseph and told Pharaoh. Joseph was again used by God to interpret yet another dream; however, this time God used it to elevate him as second in command to Pharaoh in Egypt. At once the fulfilment of Joseph's dream came to pass, being over his brothers. In fact, by the time his brothers became a witness of this reality (Joseph's new position), Joseph's mother had died, and he now had a younger brother that he had not met because of what his brothers plotted against him years before out of anger and jealousy. WOW! When we pick up the story in Genesis 50:20 we see that Joseph would have had to surrender to God our Father a lot of pain, hurt, trauma, and unforgiveness towards his brothers to get to this place where he could say these pivotal words:

> *"But as for you, you meant evil against me; but God meant it for good, in order to bring it about as it is this day, to save many people alive."*

To see beyond the visible (circumstances, the pain, the loss) and see into the invisible (His motive, His love, His strategy, His heart) prevented Joseph from embracing a murderous heart. Instead, He was humbled by the privilege to be in the position to be able to help his family. Joseph suffered and lost a lot in nearly 14 years of separation from his family. Yet, by God's grace, He was transformed into a man of valour and was elevated to fulfil his destiny. This was because he did not dwell in his circumstances, producing a murderous heart; but Joseph was able to SEE BEYOND and see the Hand of God. Despite the pain, he succumbed. His yielding resulted in

Joseph being able to demonstrate the grace, the love, the hope he had received in spite of the hardships he had faced at the hands of his brothers.

Jesus knew the dangers of developing a murderous heart so much so that He encourages us in this way: He says forget about what others will think of you or say about you when you are at the altar to give your offering and you remember that someone has something against you (emphasis mine, paraphrased from Matthew 5:23-24). In fact, Jesus emphasizes we should be intentional, leaving whatever offering we had at the altar, going and finding the person, seeking to reconcile. Unfortunately, many of us are afraid to face the emotions of pain we will face and are not quick to be honest about the offence. The fear of rejection, the feelings of inadequacy from not being honoured bring resentment, causing our insides to develop bitter waters which can result in our speaking badly about another person. All of this, results in us KILLING SOMEONE. Jesus unveils the secret to not killing. That secret is for us to take note of and embrace the ways in which He loves and forgives us, seeing only Himself and not what we do. Then be the expression of that love to others.

Recently, I have encountered every negative emotion known to man including hate. As a result, I have been concerned sometimes, with this anger and rage inside, I will open my mouth to speak and misrepresent or slander the character of someone because of the state of my heart. With the help of the Holy Spirit, I have been learning how to deal with negative emotions through honest communication, firstly with our Lord Jesus and then with others by expressing my needs and my feelings. This honesty has empowered me to see, hear and speak without judgement. Sometimes I get it wrong, but it always goes back to being honest about my needs and my feelings.

The fact that the Lord encourages us not to kill implies that He is that safe place that we can come to and seek refuge; the healing we need from negative emotion. He does not want us to walk around with the desire to kill because of anger. We can nestle in Him and remind ourselves of how He sees us, causing us to be transparent with our hearts, bearing our souls. When we look at our Bridegroom, there are numerous times He could have killed the stiff-necked Pharisees, His disciple Judas who gave Him a kiss to point Him out to His killers or His three disciples who bailed on Him when He needed them the most by sleeping. Yet His words were always Spirit and Life. Jesus knew what was in a man and He put no confidence in it. John 2:23-25 tells us this:

> *"Now when He was in Jerusalem at the Passover feast, many believed in His name [identifying themselves with Him] after seeing His signs (attesting miracles) which He was doing. But Jesus, for His part, did not entrust Himself to them, because He knew all people [and understood the superficiality and fickleness of human nature], and He did not need anyone to testify concerning man [and human nature], for He Himself knew what was in man [in their hearts—in the very core of their being]."*

Upon reading this, my understanding is our Lord knows how we gravitate towards the temporary because of us inherently eating from The Tree of the Knowledge of Good and Evil. He knows this has resulted in us being superficial, being drawn to what looks good, the by-products of this tree. He knows that partakers of The Tree of the Knowledge of Good and Evil can only manifest death. So, He came to reveal to us that He is the tree we should eat from, The Tree of Life. When we partake of Him as our life, we become impotent to kill. We begin to perceive people, their behaviour and their words differently. We too will see it is because of what is in them or because of what they are partaking of (The Tree of the Knowledge of Good and Evil) and show mercy. We will spontaneously choose to perceive, hear, feel and discern from the perspective He has shown us as we are awakened to the life of Christ in us. As the Apostle Paul puts it:

"So from now on we regard no one from a human point of view [according to worldly standards and values]. Though we have known Christ from a human point of view, now we no

> **longer know Him in this way. (2 Corinthians 5:16)**

When we see others through the eyes of love, we are moved by Love Himself and we become dead to killing, awakened to Life - the very life of God.

Cultivating Bridal Intimacy

What are the ways in which you see the love of the Bridegroom in your life?

*

Are you practicing this same expression of love to others?

*

What do you do with negative emotions? Do you suppress them?

*

Do you believe this scripture?
"And we know that all things work together for good to those who love God, to those who are the called according to His purpose." (Romans 8:28)

*

How are you practicing seeing beyond your current circumstances rather than dwelling in the pain of the

past?

*

Immerse yourself in His love for you and choose to be slow and intentional to respond as He responds to you.

Chapter 7

AWAKENING YOU TO KNOW YOU ARE THE APPLE OF HIS EYE

"Thou shalt not commit adultery"

"I Am your Source. Look to no other. I Am your

provision."

- BRIDEGROOM

Adultery is one of the greatest pains I have ever felt. It is a confirmation of betrayal, deception and disillusionment in one. It results in insecurity, anger, rage, bitterness, resentment and can potentially cause a murderous heart. The sting of adultery, if left without healing, can potentially seep into your soul causing catastrophic effects. Many have taken their lives and the lives of their adulterer both physically, emotionally, psychologically, verbally and have withered spiritually because of the sheer impact of adultery.

The online dictionary defines adultery as, "voluntary sexual intercourse between a married person and a person who is not their spouse." This is true; however, Jesus also defines adultery as looking at another with lust (a strong intense longing for another). Meanwhile, Jesus warns us and encourages us to deal with wandering eyes seriously! So much so, He said it is better to lose that one eye than your whole body. So we see that this was a topic of concern for our Bridegroom and it should be a concern for us too.

"You have heard that it was said, 'You shall not commit adultery'; but I say to you that everyone who looks at a woman with lust for her has already committed adultery with her in his heart. If your right eye makes you stumble, tear it out and throw it from you; for it is better for you to lose one of the parts of your body, than for your whole body to be thrown into hell. If your right hand makes you stumble, cut it off and throw it from you; for it is better for you to lose one of the parts of your body, than for your whole body to go into hell." (Matthew 5:27-30)

My understanding of this scripture is, anything that causes us to look outside of God as our source, can result in fatal consequences to the person looking outside of God because these consequences will be similar to the heart break incurred when a spouse has been unfaithful in a marriage. Let's go a bit deeper.

What is a source? It is a place, person, or thing from which something originates or can be obtained. Salmon is the source of fish oil. The hose on the other hand is not the source of water. The hose is simply the carrier of the water. When we put our faith in the hose rather than the original source of the water, this leads to unreasonable expectations causing disappointments and hopelessness. So it is when we put our faith in a resource over our only SOURCE. When we do this, we are being adulterous. In my experience of adultery, I would even be as bold to say, the pains of adultery are even more devastating to those who have sought to put their faith in a resource (a person, a thing, an opportunity) *sent by God* rather than The Source of the resource (GOD HIMSELF).

I pray we will be able to identify quickly when our faith is misplaced. Until our attitude towards a resource is seeing it as a conduit of God, only then will we know we are captivated by our only TRUE Source. He has our eyes, they are fixed solely on Him. He alone can truly satisfy. Another way to see this is essentially people can only give from what they have or, in spiritual terms, from the capacity to which they have been awakened. If they are only awakened to two percent of their love capacity but you are demanding 100% you will be heartbroken because you are demanding from someone who may only have one apple, but you are demanding 50 apples. This will always make the person with the expectation feel disillusioned and want to retaliate by expressing anger, manipulation, or threats but unfortunately none of those inspire or bring about change. Instead this results in the devastation of heartbreak.

Our Bridegroom wants us to understand His proposal to us, "Do not commit adultery." He wants us to understand that He is our Source. Colossians 1:16 puts it this way:

> *"For by him all things were created, in heaven and on earth, visible and invisible, whether thrones or dominions or rulers or authorities— all things were created through him and for him."*

And the Apostle John says it this way:

> *"All things came into being through Him, and apart from Him nothing came into being that*

has come into being." (John 1:3)

These scriptures reiterate the truth that He is the Author and Perfecter, Alpha and Omega so all things start or originate with Him and end with Him.

Jesus sets us a remarkable example as He only looked to the Father as His Source. He demonstrated numerous times that the Father was central to who He is - His identity, His purpose and His character.

> *"I can do nothing on My own initiative. As I hear, I judge; and My judgment is just, because I do not seek My own will, but the will of Him who sent Me."* (John 5:30)

> *"If you keep My commandments, you will abide in My love; just as I have kept My Father's commandments and abide in His love."* (John

15:10)

"Truly, truly, I say to you, the Son can do nothing of Himself, unless it is something He sees the Father doing; for whatever the Father does, these things the Son also does in like manner. (John 5:19)

Jesus said to him, "Have I been so long with you, and yet you have not come to know Me, Philip? He who has seen Me has seen the Father; how can you say, 'Show us the Father.' (John 14:9)

You can see from all these scriptures, and there are many more, that Jesus looked only to the Father and saw His identity only in the Father. The Father was His ONLY SOURCE. He was confident of His eternal victory, He was resourceful when there was a lack. When He was faced with manipulation, He spoke the words of His Father. When He faced betrayal, He saw beyond the betrayer and asked His Father to:

> *"forgive them for they know not what they do…"* **(Luke 23:24)**

When He faced false authority, being aware there was only One authority and One power and One order, He was confident they were subjected to Him but refused to use His power unless His Father, our PAPA, willed it. He said:

> *"Or do you think that I cannot appeal to My Father, and He will at once put at My disposal more than twelve legions of angels."* **(Matthew 26:52)**

Knowing His authority, *"**Jesus answered, 'You would have no authority over Me, unless it had**

been given you from above; for this reason he who delivered Me to you has the greater sin.'"
(John 19:11)

The Father was the Source of His power and He would not use it unless given the go ahead by the Father.

You see that by this very commandment, "Do not commit adultery," it is not only our Bridegroom's commitment of being faithful to His Bride no matter what; a commitment He demonstrated in every aspect of His life on earth. But it is also the secret to not being entangled with unforgiveness, offense, murder and resentment, the very entanglements that hinder us from manifesting Love Himself. Essentially, the hurt, disillusionment, disappointment, and indifference we face is rooted in looking to others as the source rather than the TRUE SOURCE. When we stop looking for affirmation from people, we are beginning to walk in freedom to be faithful first to our only SOURCE, our MANUFACTURER and our POINT OF ORIGIN, then committing adultery does not become a temptation. For, after all, you were made *for Him*.

Cultivating Bridal Intimacy

What resources have you been treating like your source?

*

What is a source?

*

Who is your Source?

*

Is your heart captivated by your Source? If not, ask Him to captivate your heart.

*

Because you have Christ, you have been given all you need. When you carry the Source, you stop looking outside of yourself and draw from within.

Chapter 8

AWAKENING YOU TO HIM BEING YOUR SOURCE OF ALL THINGS

"Do not steal"

"All I have Is yours."

- BRIDEGROOM

The word *steal* is defined as taking something that is not yours. If all He has is yours and He has it all, why would we steal? The answer is simple, *unbelief.* Lack is a lie geared to cause disillusionment. When that became apparent to me, I was gobsmacked! However, I felt impotent to change my mindset that had been immersed in the lie that, *if I did not see the manifestation of the money I needed, I did not have any.* One night while sleeping, I had a series of night visions all evoking the same message: "LACK IS AN ILLUSION". The problem I was having was my intellect was stopping me from receiving the revelation. I did not see it. Isn't faith belief in the unseen? So, because you cannot see it, this is not a reason to believe in lack. Ephesians 1:3 says:

> *"Blessed be the God and Father of our Lord Jesus Christ, who has blessed us with every spiritual blessing in the heavenly places in Christ."*

Everything is spiritual and scripture says we have been given *every spiritual blessing*, but... where is it? It is in the heavenly places in Christ. Where is that? In you and in me. So you see, if we are looking outwardly, our intellect, our ability to reason and to be logical, will prevent us from looking inside and drawing from within, instead we will look aimlessly on the seen, the exterior.

The Bible presents to us a story of a father who had two sons. When we look at the story of the prodigal son, one could deduce the younger son only wanted what His Father had. He was not interested in a relationship with his father. So, he demanded from his father all of his inheritance and went and lived as an orphan squandering all he had. The older son, though he stayed home and served his Dad, was jealous of his younger brother upon his return as he was being showered with gifts, because he was totally unaware of his own rights and privileges as a son. He was not conscious of the blessings that came with whose he was. He was jealous of his brother because he felt he was more responsible, yet he did not get this extravagant treatment. He qualified himself for this extravagance based on the fact that he was present, he was faithful and he was responsible. Comparison made the older son feel unworthy and feel frustrated that though he thought he had earned his father's inheritance, he had received nothing. Both sons were very orphaned in their hearts. They had their father and were heirs, but they lacked a conscious awareness of the wealth that had no end. This was the endless supply of unconditional acceptance and love that would silence the need to make your own way as the younger brother attempted or the need to serve from a place of duty and religious pride as the older brother proved to be just as futile. The two brothers were yet to be awakened to their identity as sons of their father and its implications. I believe in many ways this is a true picture of many of us today.

This is what the father said when he saw the dilemma:

"Son, you are always with me, and all that I have is yours." **(Luke 15:31)**

I believe this is the heart of the Father for us and as Jesus our Bridegroom said, *"when you see me you see the Father."* So, Jesus was an expression of Who the Father is. The word *always* in the first statement implies there *has been no time, no space, no separation between the son and the Father at any time.* WOAH! In the second part of the statement, the word *all* in the Hebrew and the

117

Greek is still *all*; all encompassing. It includes anything you think the word *all* would include. According to Jesus' parable, **"all that I have is yours,"** reveals to us the Fathers heart and His heart as our Bridegroom: *"My power, My knowledge, My heart, My thoughts, My love, My resources are all yours."* If you are married, then you know legally all your husband or wife has is yours. So, it is in the Spirit. All Jesus your Bridegroom has is yours. Hence why begging and pleading in the place of prayer is pointless, it is a clear sign of UNBELIEF! When we beg for what we already have, it is a sign that we are not awakened to this truth - *lack is an illusion*. It is time to call forth the manifestation of what is already ours. In my experience, we cannot manifest what we have not awakened to, hence the need to meditate on this truth or reality.

Jesus demonstrated over and over again that He lacked nothing. He had whatever He needed. If it were knowledge, He listened and saw what the Father showed Him and spoke accordingly. If He needed money, He sent the disciples to fetch the money from the fish's mouth. When He needed food, the little food that was given He gave thanks to the Father and He multiplied it. When He felt weak, angels were sent to strengthen Him. Whatever He needed, He knew how to access it. He was never hopeless.

In recent years, I found myself responding in fear and anxiety at the sign of any seeming lack. I believe this was a manifestation of a traumatic time we went through several years ago financially, which resulted in me wondering where and how we would live. It was a time of hardship and despair and, though our Father worked it all out for our good, my memories needed healing. However, when I breathe slowly and intentionally remind myself of Whose I am, and the incredible access I have, immediately my soul is restored. My shallow breathing of anxiety becomes full deep breaths that keep me calm and full of faith in He Who is my Provider. Jesus did not believe in lack because He knew who His Daddy was and that He could not lack with the Shepherd as His Father.

Another way to look at 'stealing' is to carry a burden that is not yours. Jesus said it this way:

> *"Come to me, all you who are weary and burdened, and I will give you rest. Take my yoke (His teaching, His perspective) upon you and learn from me, for I am gentle and humble."* (Matthew 11:28-30)

JESUS IS OUR BURDEN BEARER. To carry burdens

that are not light is to steal from our Burden Bearer what He is to be carrying. Jesus is inevitably telling us to live our lives light. Seeking to live like this is really to live a life of surrender, constantly seeking out the perspective of our Bridegroom.

Living light is to live from above, the only way to live. When we are burdened by life and its circumstances, this weighs us down causing us to live from below rather than from above. The Apostle Paul says it this way:

> *"...you were raised with Christ, seek those things which are above, where Christ is, sitting at the right hand of God. Set your mind on things above, not on things on the earth."* **(Colossians 3:1-2)**

So, we see that there is a mindset of living above that is indictive of what our minds are set on. It encourages us to set our minds on things that are above (unseen eternal) not on the earth (the seen, the temporary) things.

Jesus was found many times away from the crowd engaging His Father. Jesus lived from above. As a result, overthinking, anxiety, worrying, fear, unforgiveness, offence were not habits He had. He could not afford a thought outside of our Father's, neither can we. Jesus knew that as a man thinks so is he, so he becomes, so he manifests. In other words, man can only manifest what he thinks. I believe a lot of His alone time was to align with the perspective and the narrative of our Father.

We see Jesus in the Garden of Gethsemane, burdened by His inevitable sacrifice. His first inclination was to separate Himself to seek His Father's perspective. He took His three best friends but left them to pray as He went off on His own to empty Himself of what He knew would be a great hardship. The Bible recalls that He prayed for some time and then He said:

> *"Behold, the hour is at hand, and the Son of Man is being betrayed into the hands of sinners (Those who knew what they were doing). Rise, let us be going. See, My betrayer is at hand."*
> **(Matthew 26:45-46)**

Jesus was so light or burden free, He did not hide from His betrayer, He did not run away. He got up and decisively was ready to face what was to come. This is a powerful example of Jesus mirroring for us how to live light. *Do not steal.* Throw off the lies of lack and its illusion. Throw off the burden of life and its circumstances and put them on the Lover of your Soul; your Burden Bearer.

One of Jesus disciples, Peter, the disciple who was well known for his independent thinking (so much so that it led to his denial of our Lord), had this to say after his many failures:

> **"Casting all your cares [all your anxieties, all your worries, and all your concerns, once and for all] on Him, for He cares about you [with deepest affection, and watches over you very carefully].** (1 Peter 5:7)

So you see, there is an invitation to live a life that is light. In this life free of burdens, you will not steal because it opens your eyes to see your provision from the Kingdom within you. Ambassadors will always look to the place they represent. As representors of God, your provision is within you, *the Christ in you.*

Cultivating Bridal Intimacy

Does your prayer life show a belief in the truth that you have no lack?

*

Do you find yourself overthinking?

*

Why not replace it with living a life of surrender...

*

Worry does not change tomorrow, it takes away

your peace for today.

Live light and soar like the eagle you are.

Chapter 9

AWAKENING YOU TO HIS HEART AND PERCEPTION

"Do not bear false witness"

"My words and I are one; no separation.

My words carry My heart. It is the only Truth."

- BRIDEGROOM

"Thou shall not bear false witness against your neighbour." (Exodus 20:16)

When I read this statement I wondered how I would define a false witness. My spontaneous response is someone who concocts stories that are not true with the intention to discredit or defame a person's character. I believe that is true. When I asked the Holy Spirit what would He considers to be a false witness, He added, *"False witnesses take what you have said and twist it rather than grasp the heart by which it was said."* Matthew 26: 59-63 is a great example of this:

> *"Now the chief priests and the whole council were seeking false testimony against Jesus that they might put him to death, but they found none, though many false witnesses came forward. At last two came forward and said, "This man said, 'I am able to destroy the temple*

of God, and to rebuild it in three days.' And the high priest stood up and said, 'Have you no answer to make? What is it that these men testify against you?' But Jesus remained silent."

Here these false witnesses repeated what Jesus said but clearly misunderstood the symbolic language He used. By their own misconception they agreed with the lie; their belief contributed to His crucifixion.

We see the effects of lies and how they hold others captive, or ransomed by way of accusation, slander and judgement. On the other hand, when we embrace truth it sets us free and others too. If the people who heard Jesus speak about rebuilding the temple in three days had no preconceived judgements of Jesus, they would not have heard further evidence to judge and crucify Him. This is a lesson for us all. The Bible says it this way:

"The pure in heart will see God." (Matthew 5:8)

A pure heart will see the God in a person over what they do or even what they say. Some time ago, I was looking at the numerous times that Jesus encouraged us to be like children. As I inquired of Him about how He perceives a child, He explained that a child trusts, causing them to abide in His love, feeling no need to prove their worth through attaining. A child has no pre-conceived ideas. When we have no judgments of others, we are able to hear with discernment rather than our own prejudices. These false witnesses were unable to hear Jesus' heart and to deduce correctly His intention because they already had ill motives and intentions, towards Him.

Lying of any kind, when traced, always seems to be

rooted in fear; fear of the unknown, fear of rejection, fear of abandonment, fear of being alone, fear of being different, fear of not being enough. So, one could say lying is the fruit of fear when lies are presented and believed. Being a false witness starts with fear and not knowing who you are, resulting in insecurity, jealousy and a potentially murderous heart. Essentially, this is what happened to these false witnesses. They felt threatened by Jesus' new teachings and felt displaced in their social and religious standing. Therefore, they would do and say anything to undermine Him or cause His followers to scatter. We see this in the scripture above, but we certainly see this in our everyday lives, in our making slight remarks, or asking questions to instigate wrong views about others. When we see our value only from the eyes of our Bridegroom, we live our lives from inside out. This means we do not allow ourselves to be seeking gratification about our value, our beauty, our worth from external factors. These external factors can be relationships, social status, money, education, children, marriage and the like. When our security, our safe place, is in our Bridegroom Christ alone, we climb off of the emotional roller coaster. We prevent ourselves from feeling used and abused by people when we are awakened to trust the motive and intention of our Bridegroom. His motive towards us is always love. His intention is always for us to fulfil destiny. He told me some time ago, *"I have never had a bad thought about you."* Hmmm, I remember thinking I am so far from that. Unfortunately, we have been immersed in a culture of judgment which leads to slander and false witnessing. So, the idea of not having a bad thought of someone seems foreign. Yet scripture is clear that:

"As He (Jesus) is so are we," (1 John 4:17b)

Therefore, we can think only the best of others. Being a recipient of His love erases the need to fear; hence, dispels the need to slander and ultimately become a false witness. A person who is consciously aware of how loved, valued, and treasured they are will only seek His best for others.

> *"This is My commandment, that you love one another as I have loved you."* (John 15:12)

The word commandment is perceived by Jews not as a burdensome task but as a way to express our gratitude. A contrast to our view of commandment. So, when we obey His commandment of loving the way God loves us it is an expression of our gratitude to Him and His treatment of us. Jesus encourages us to love one another as He has loved us. So, this love is not our version of love, but we are to take note of the ways Jesus expresses His love to us and be that way for others. When I began to actively do this, I really saw how we enjoy receiving love, but we are not as quick to love in the same way.

> *"Love the Lord your God with all your heart and with all your soul and with all your mind and with all your strength. The second is this: 'Love your neighbour as yourself.'"* (Mark 12:30-31)

Love your neighbour as you love yourself implies to us that we cannot think of loving anyone if we do not first love ourselves. This also means how you perceive yourself is how you will perceive others. What we see in others are easily the very things we reject and hate about ourselves. This is why the scripture encourages us to love God as He loves us but to love others the way we love ourselves. Many times, we spontaneously do the reverse. We try to love God before being consciously aware of how He loves us. It is hard to believe this extravagant love He has for us first. We try to love others before we first love ourselves. This backward thinking always results in frustration and a burden or pressure to perform. His perspective of being a conscious recipient first, always reveals to others His love.

Someone who is constantly late can look at someone who never honours their word and judge them as lacking integrity, when really it is the same lack of integrity being exposed in being late as in not honouring your word. This is what happens when we judge others because we sin differently. It is not only hypocritical, it is seeing through the wrong lens. Until we see our lack of integrity in being late and surrender it to God in humility, only then do we respond without judgment towards someone who is not keeping their word. Then we can be more compassionate not to leave them in this, but to hold their hand and walk together in love. Years ago, the Lord whispered to my heart.

"Christine, you can judge, or you can love, but you cannot do both." It silenced me then. What say you?

Our Bridegroom loves us. He does not judge our behaviours. If He did, He would not have given Himself as a sacrifice for all people. The following incidents show how He did not judge behaviours. People He called friends, even in the midst of His surrender, were sleeping when he needed them to pray. He would not have allowed Judas to kiss him as a sign of his betrayal of Him. He would not have healed the soldier whose ear Peter cut off in the midst of being arrested. If Jesus judged by appearances, He would not have asked in the midst of being rejected, scorned and mutilated:

> *"...Father, forgive them; for they know not what they are doing..."* **(Luke 23:34)**

Jesus lived His life listening to the heart of people and challenged people on the state of their hearts. He judged people purely by Whose they are: HIS. Always calling us to His bride, His workmanship, His people, He gave all despite our resistance so we can see ourselves the way He sees us. The sacrifice on the cross shouts, how valuable, perfect, redeemed, justified, holy, and worthy He sees us. These are only a few words that describe the results of His act of love. I believe not bearing false witness starts with us seeing our Bridegroom as He is, seeing ourselves the way He sees us, and seeing others and our circumstances, not from superficial appearances, but seeing them as He sees them.

If you are honest, you will see we are all guilty of bearing false witness. Any false perception of God, first and foremost, sets us up to believe and empower lies about Him and thus ourselves.

Without a doubt, believing false images about ourselves taints our view of others. This prevents us from seeing people as His image and His likeness, causing us to see others based on what we see in their behaviour.

Cultivating Bridal Intimacy

What false images of God do you carry?

*

What false images of yourself have you accepted?

*

What false images of others have you accepted?

*

Listen without judgment. Refuse to be captivated by

appearances, see from within.

Jesus said be careful how you listen... This suggests

to us there is a way that we listen that can cause us

to perceive wrongly which can cause us to be a false

witness.

Chapter 10

AWAKENING YOU TO HIS TRUE IMAGE, RELINQUISHING ALL FALSE IMAGE OF GOD

"Do not covet"

"Gratitude silences covetousness."

- BRIDEGROOM

We live in a world where everyone is trying to make it. It is a rat race. Covetousness is fuelling the race, "I want what this one has." Culture has set a false measuring stick or false reference point, of what success looks like which causes many to feel inadequate and causes striving to fuel covetousness.

The question is though: Who sets the benchmark of what true success looks like? I believe only the Author and the Perfecter can. It would seem the death, the resurrection and ascension of Jesus Christ are God's view of success. By these three life changing events, perception of true success was veiled because you and I were also dead, resurrected and raised with Him. By this, everything that was done by the first Adam was undone by the Last Adam, our Bridegroom. Success is awakening to what is already done and walking in its reality.

Covetousness is an unawareness of what has always been from the foundation of the world. The Apostle Paul said it this way:

"...just as [in His love] He chose us in Christ [actually selected us for Himself as His own] before the foundation of the world, so that we would be holy [that is, consecrated, set apart for Him, purpose-driven] and blameless in His sight. In love." **(Ephesians 1:4)**

We see that we were *chosen, handpicked, favoured, decided on, espoused, appointed, named and adopted* before the foundation of the world. That spells success for me; set apart as His very own.

When we are unaware of what we have, we begin to develop wandering eyes. Eyes that wander are consumed with all that everyone else has but are unable to see what they possess. When our eyes are fixated on what we do not have (or have not seen), we cannot appreciate how much we have in the unseen. Only what is the unseen will last or is eternal. If what you think you have you can see, it is temporary, and it will pass away. I once heard someone say, 'comparison is a thief of time.' The majority of the time comparison gives birth to envy, jealousy, competitiveness and an inability to see or desire the best for others. Although, comparison does not have to be negative, it can also inspire others to develop and grow.

It was covetousness, envy, jealousy and comparison that caused the death of Abel, the selling of Joseph, the stealing of Esau's birthright. Covetousness is self-absorbed and seeks to be always looking for opportunities for self, whilst feeling threatened by others. Those who are not intimately acquainted with or immersed into their rights and privileges as a son or a daughter revel in covetousness. This results in selfish ambition or trying to make it on our own, or a willingness to gauge someone else's eyes out so they will not make it or go further than you.

The Bible tells us of a story of ten lepers, let's read:

Now on his way to Jerusalem, Jesus travelled along the border between Samaria and Galilee. As he was going into a village, ten men who had leprosy met him. They stood at a distance and called out in a loud voice, "Jesus, Master, have pity on us!" When he saw them, he said, "Go, show yourselves to the priests." And as they went, they were cleansed. One of them, when he saw he was healed, came back, praising God in a loud voice. He threw himself at Jesus' feet and thanked him—and he was a Samaritan. Jesus asked, "Were not all ten

cleansed? Where are the other nine? Has no one returned to give praise to God except this foreigner?" Then he said to him, "Rise and go; your faith has made you well." (Luke 17:11-19)

One could deduce that these lepers knew of Jesus' ability to heal and, as a result, intercepted Him as He entered and greeted Him with 'honour' in order for Jesus to favour them. We could question whether this was mainly because of what they wanted from Him, not because they wanted a relationship with Him. They wanted what He had. Too often we see that when we embraced false identity about ourselves it causes us to misuse others. False identity blinds us to our true value and so hustling others becomes a way of life. One can then deduce that these nine lepers had embraced a false identity of themselves. Scripture does not say how long they had been lepers. We do not know if they were born like this. We have always been in the habit of associating our identity with what we do or not do. So, we could deduce that these lepers saw themselves as just lepers and the treatment that came with that title.

History shows that lepers were isolated by society at large. They were scorned, they were the dejected, rejected and abandoned by their community. So, you can imagine that these 10 lepers were probably relieved to have had the stigma of a leper be lifted from them. There is a saying we have in Jamaica, "You can bring the cow to the water but you cannot make him drink". This is what I believe happened to these 9 lepers. I believe though they were healed, and they were pronounced healed by the priest, they still carried the shame, the condemnation and the judgement that they had lived under for years. Though they were healed they did not embrace the full freedom that comes with being free from the oppression that comes with being a leper.

A good example of this, is with the people of Israel and their enslavement in Egypt for many, many years. Yet, years later they were freed by God through a man God trained and equipped called Moses. We see, that whenever there was a hurdle or a circumstance that seemed unfavourable, the Israelites grumbled, complained, sometimes desiring to go back to the confinement, the oppression they once knew. It is sad. Yet, I do not believe this is limited to these nine lepers or to the children of Israel. What we see today in ourselves, how we engage with life, the ingratitude we express or live out is from the same issue at hand. The legendary Bob Marley says it this way, "Emancipate yourself from mental slavery. None but our selves can free our minds." Bob Marley identified the problem, mental slavery, but knew not the solution. Jesus our Bridegroom is the only Solution. He came to show us how to live free. The Apostle Paul describes transformation as a renewal of the mind. I would also say true gratitude finds its origin in a renewal of our mind, letting go of all that trained us to think and behave, like slaves. True transformation for us all has been a spiritual progression because revelation is progressive. Transformation begins when we see ourselves the way God sees us. When I see myself through His eyes it changes how I see myself. This changes my thoughts and inevitably it changes my behaviour. Consequentially, it changes my circumstances; then, it changes my life and the way I live. This is transformation; it starts from the mind.

You see, the 10 lepers experienced healing, a miraculous restoration that day, but only one came back and expressed His gratitude. When you truly know (awaken to) how oppressed you were and how it affected you emotionally, spiritually, psychologically, only then can you truly appreciate your freedom when it comes. If not, you will always look back through your eyes and be delusional by what you perceived. When you see your oppression the way God sees it, that your Bridegroom, saw it fit to leave divinity to be our ultimate sacrifice to set you and I free, then gratitude would be our spontaneous response not regret, covetousness nor ingratitude. Covetousness is looking back at what was, what could have been, what might have been. It is a form of illusion manifested in regrets. This mindset prevents us from manifesting the image and likeness of the God who created us and made us His very own. When we look back, may we be sure to look back through the eyes of Him who did all that was possible for us to be free preventing us to assume the false image of covetousness. Gratitude says I know what I have been freed from and I cannot afford to look to the right nor the left. Let our eyes be fixed on Him who saw it fit to make you His own: My Bridegroom, Your Bridegroom; *Jesus.*

Cultivating Bridal Intimacy

Consider writing out what you know you have been saved from.

*

Identify the ways you have been showing ingratitude and remember from where you have come.

*

Practice looking through the eyes of Jesus, whether you look back or gaze on the present.

*

Be conscious of your oneness with Him. See through His eyes, hear from His perspective, feel what He feels, discern what He discerns. In Him you live and move and have your being.

AWAKENING YOU TO YOUR COMPLETENESS, YOUR PERFECTION, YOUR INNOCENCE IN HIM

Being one with His proposal

When we see ourselves separate from Jesus we will always feel burdened by any instruction of His. When He speaks, He is always speaking oneness. He is always speaking with no separation between us and Him. This is why scripture says:

> *"I can do all things through Christ who strengthens me."* (Philippians 4:13)

Speaking of this oneness we have with Him that empowers us in all things. In John 6:33-37 we see the same theme of oneness:

> *"For the bread of God is He who comes down from heaven and gives life to the world." Then they said to Him, "Lord, give us this bread always. And Jesus said to them, "I am the bread of life. He who comes to Me shall never hunger, and he who believes in Me shall never thirst."*

Jesus is saying here, to partake of Him and all that He is in us - the Bread of Life - is to be satisfied. It is to be awakened to who He is and who He came to show us about ourselves in Him.

- *"I am the Lord thy God, thou shalt not have any strange gods before Me."* I HAVE MADE YOU MY PRIORITY, I SO VALUE YOU I GAVE YOU MY LIFE, MY COMMITMENT IS FULLY IRREVOCABLE.

- *"Thou shalt not take the name of the Lord thy God in vain."* MY NAME REVEALS MY HEART, MY NATURE, MY CHARACTER. TO BE AWAKENED TO THE ONENESS YOU HAVE WITH MY NAME YOU CANNOT MISREPRESENT ME.

- *"Remember to keep holy the Sabbath day."* WILL YOU GIVE ME ONE DAY THAT IS MY DAY WITH YOU TO HEAL AND RESTORE? WILL YOU BE SO AWARE OF MY EVERPRESENCE THAT YOU RULE OVER THE SABBATH AND NOT LET IT RULE YOU.

- *"Honour thy father and mother."* YOUR FATHER AND MOTHER ARE A SHADOW OF

WHO I AM. TO HONOUR THOSE YOU CAN SEE PREPARES YOU TO HONOUR THE UNSEEN (ME).

- *"Thou shall not kill."* BRING TO ME YOUR THOUGHTS OF HATE, ANGER, RAGE, SLANDER, (MURDEROUS HEART). I CAN GIVE YOU MY PERSPECTIVE AND RESTORE YOU TO RAISE THE DEAD BECAUSE THAT IS YOUR RIGHT, YOUR PRIVILEDGE AS MY BRIDE.

- *"Thou shall not commit adultery."* WILL YOU ALLOW YOUR EYES TO BE SO CAPTIVATED BY ME AS YOUR ONLY SOURCE THAT YOU DO NOT LOOK TO ANOTHER?

- *"Thou shall not steal."* WILL YOU ALLOW ME TO BE YOUR BURDEN BEARER? LAY EVERY BURDEN ON ME: MY BACK IS BROAD ENOUGH; MY ARMS ARE WIDE ENOUGH. TO CARRY WHAT I AM TO CARRY; IS STEALING.

- *"Thou shall not bear false witness against*

your neighbour." LOVE THE WAY I LOVE YOU. LISTEN TO THE HEART OF WHAT OTHERS ARE SAYING SO THAT YOU CAN JUDGE AS I JUDGE. TREAT OTHERS NOT BASED ON THEIR BEHAVIOUR BUT WHAT THEY ARE WORTH.

- *"Thou shall not covet."* I HAVE GIVEN YOU ALL THINGS. I HAVE SET YOU UP AS A RULER AND MASTER OVER ALL. WALK IN THIS REALITY AND BE GRATEFUL.

Will you embrace My love? I am awakening you to My bridal proposal to move you from *Chav* (a one-sided love) to *Racham* (a two-sided love). When our hearts spontaneously reciprocate His love by believing and walking as Christ Himself, His awakening spontaneously causes our hearts to be Christ conscious as it is immersed in His love for you and me.

SCRIPTURES TO MEDITATE ON

Awakening to His love

"For, lo, the winter is past, the rain is over and gone;
The flowers appear on the earth; the time of the
singing of birds is come, and the voice of the turtle is
heard in our land."
(Song of Solomon 2:11-12)

*

"Return, return, O Shulamite; Return, return, that we
may look upon you!"
(Song of Solomon 6:13)

*

"For God so loved the world that he gave his one and
only Son, that whoever believes in him shall not perish

but have eternal life."

(John 3:16)

*

"Greater love has no one than this: to lay down one's

life for one's friends."

(John 15:13)

*

"Above all, love each other deeply, because love

covers over a multitude of sins."

(1 Peter 4:8)

*

"But God demonstrates his own love for us in this:

While we were still sinners, Christ died for us."

(Romans 5:8)

"But you, O Lord, are a compassionate and gracious God, slow to anger, abounding in love and faithfulness."

(Psalm 86:15)

*

"Let all that you do be done in love."

(1 Corinthians 16:14)

*

"So now I am giving you a new commandment: Love each other. Just as I have loved you, you should love each other. Your love for one another will prove to the world that you are my disciples."

(John 13:34-35)

*

"There is no fear in love. But perfect love drives out

161

fear, because fear has to do with punishment. The one who fears is not made perfect in love. We love because He first loved us."

(1 John 4:18-19)

*

"So now faith, hope, and love abide, these three; but the greatest of these is love."

(1 Corinthians 13:13)

*

"If you love me, you will obey what I command."

(John 14:15)

*

Beyond all these things put on and wrap yourselves in [unselfish] love, which is the perfect bond of unity [for everything is bound together in agreement when each one seeks the best for others].

(Colossians 3:14)

*

"Dear friends, let us love one another, for love comes from God. Everyone who loves has been born of God and knows God.   Whoever does not love does not know God, because God is love."

(1 John 4:7-8)

*

"Hate stirs up trouble, but love forgives all offenses."

(Proverbs 10:12)

*

"Love must be sincere. Hate what is evil; cling to what is good. Be devoted to one another in brotherly love. Honour one another above yourselves."

(Romans 12:9-10)

*

"Give thanks to the Lord, for he is good; his love
endures forever."
(1 Chronicles 16:34)

"A friend loves at all times, and a brother is born for a
time of adversity."
(Proverbs 17:17)

*

"The Lord your God is with you, he is mighty to save.
He will take great delight in you, he will quiet you with
his love, he will rejoice over you with singing."
(Zephaniah 3:17)

*

"He has shown you, O man, what is good. And what does the Lord require of you? To act justly and to love mercy and to walk humbly with your God."
(Micah 6:8)

*

"Be completely humble and gentle; be patient, bearing with one another in love."
(Ephesians 4:2)

*

"For Christ's love compels us, because we are convinced that one died for all, and therefore all died."
(2 Corinthians 5:14)

*

"But love your enemies, do good to them, and lend to

them without expecting to get anything back. Then

your reward will be great..."

(Luke 6:35)

*

"Husbands, love your wives, as Christ loved the church

and gave himself up for her."

(Ephesians 5:25)

*

"But you are a forgiving God, gracious and

compassionate, slow to anger and abounding in

love..."

(Nehemiah 9:17)

*

"Let them give thanks to the Lord for his unfailing love

and his wonderful deeds for men, for he satisfies the

thirsty and fills the hungry with good things."

(Psalm 107:8-9)

*

"For you have been called to live in freedom, my brothers and sisters. But don't use your freedom to satisfy your sinful nature. Instead, use your freedom to serve one another in love. For the whole law can be summed up in this one command: 'Love your neighbour as yourself.'"

(Galatians 5:13-14)

*

"But the fruit of the Spirit is love, joy, peace, patience, kindness, goodness, faithfulness, gentleness and self-control."

(Galatians 5:22-23)

*

"Owe no one anything, except to love each other, for the one who loves another has fulfilled the law."
(Romans 13:8)

*

"Your love, O Lord, reaches to the heavens, your faithfulness to the skies. Your righteousness is like the mighty mountains, your justice like the great deep."
(Psalm 36:5-6)

*

"Live a life of love, just as Christ loved us and gave himself up for us as a fragrant offering and sacrifice to God."
(Ephesians 5:2)

*

"Anyone who claims to be in the light but hates his brother is still in the darkness. Whoever loves his brother lives in the light, and there is nothing in him to make him stumble."

(1 John 2:9-10)

*

"How great is the love the Father has lavished on us, that we should be called children of God!"

(1 John 3:1)

*

"This is how we know what love is: Jesus Christ laid down his life for us. And we ought to lay down our lives for our brothers. If anyone has material possessions and sees his brother in need but has no pity on him, how can the love of God be in him? Dear children, let us not love with words or tongue but with actions and in truth."

(1 John 3:16-18)

*

"This is how God showed his love among us: He sent his one and only Son into the world that we might live through him. This is love: not that we loved God, but that he loved us and sent his Son as an atoning sacrifice for our sins. Dear friends, since God so loved us, we also ought to love one another."

(1 John 4:9-11)

*

"His banner over me is love."

(Song of Songs 2:4)

*

"The commandments...are summed up in the one command, 'Love your neighbour as you love yourself.'

If you love others, you will never do them wrong, to love, then, is to obey the whole Law."

(Romans 13:9-10)

*

BIOGRAPHY

Dr Christine Nelson is an ordained pastor, a prophetic messenger, a sought-after teacher, international speaker, radio/tv host of *Revealing the Christ in You*, songwriter, mentor, entrepreneur, Director of CN Publishing House and the author of the *Walking in Oneness* series. She is the founder and overseer of *CNMinistries* and *CN Apostolic Equipping Institute*.

She is passionate about helping people develop a relationship with God that is deep, meaningful and intimate. This passion was birthed having been brought up by a single parent. This conjured feeling of abandonment and rejection of not knowing a father's love. She became desperate to have that real knowing in her walk with God and endeavoured to "Take the Father by the Hand".

This passion has led her to equip believers to hear, know and follow God on a moment by moment experience. She teaches the foundational truth of the Word with simplicity, while revealing deep things of the spirit in practical ways. She has the unique ability to demystify the supernatural side of a real relationship with the Living God and make it an accessible reality for all believers.

Christine was called by God supernaturally. God uses her to bring His glory of transformation, to bring freedom through His prophetic teachings, deliverance, healing, supernatural encounter. Christine is a prophetic equipper. God has combined the teaching gift and the prophetic gift and has used her to equip, empower, engage as we live a supernatural lifestyle.

OTHER BOOKS BY CHRISTINE NELSON

Taking the Father by the Hand –

Walking in Oneness

Step up and Step in - *Oneness Transforms*

Seeing yourself through the Eyes of Jesus -

Oneness Personifies

Knowing Him in His Glory -

Oneness Reveals His Person

Contend for your Faith - *Oneness Discerns Truth*

Reawakening in Him - *Oneness Embodies Christ*

The Father I never knew - *Oneness Reveals Sons*

The Big Shift - *Oneness unplugs us from the Earth*

CHECK OUT THESE BOOKS ON:

WWW.CNPUBLISHINGHOUSE.COM

DO YOU HAVE A BOOK THAT YOU WANT TO PUBLISH?

Check out our competitive price plans for our book deals too.

CHECK OUT OUR ONLINE INSTITUTE:

<u>WWW.CNMAEI.COM</u>

This institute is unique in many ways. You have full access to it by any device, be it a smart phone, iPad, laptop or a computer with internet access from anywhere in the world.

We do an array of series which come packed with groundbreaking teaching, notes, life changing activations, homework and discussions.

We carry two classes per week, one class at a UK friendly time and the other USA friendly time.

CNM APOSTOLIC EQUIPPING INSTITUTE

MATURING THE SONS OF GOD!

See our upcoming courses for 2019:

- IN CHRIST REALITY – *Embracing His Life*
- HIS WORDS IN YOUR DREAMS – *Understanding Symbolic Language*
- LIVING FROM ETERNITY - *Embracing His Perspective*

"For the anxious longing of the creation waits eagerly for the revealing of the sons of God."
-Romans 8:19

CNM APOSTOLIC EQUIPPING INSTITUTE

"Maturing the Sons of God"

www.cnmaei.com

www.ingramcontent.com/pod-product-compliance
Lightning Source LLC
Chambersburg PA
CBHW071219090426
42736CB00014B/2895